"A poet whose inner life is a torrent of imagery sweeping the reader into a maelstrom on the page—frightening to experience but one continues to read, adjusting, recognizing yet another form of speech to be understood . . . and finally to enjoy with admiration for the skill with which such ferocity finds itself on a page with consistent style and force."
—DAVID IGNATOW

"Edward Butscher is one of the most accomplished of contemporary poets. . . . His poems are never opaque; he expresses his perceptions of the world in images that not only correspond to them but become a new world to themselves."
—STEPHEN STEPANCHEV

"Through the use of masks, other selves, and a sometimes gleeful, if macabre, poetic wit, Butscher journeys through growth and regression, brushing sleeves with love and death, toward the multifaceted knowledge that all good poems must dare confront."—PETER WILD

"Poetry is a sullen art, and Edward Butscher knows the etymology of the word and the true root of all art. . . . His poems are a source of strength. . . . Butscher is out for blood. His is a no-nonsense poetry, filled with our primordial origins."—SIMON PERCHIK

Local Lexicon

Published by box of chalk
www.forgejournal.com

Names: Butscher, Edward, author.
Title: Local Lexicon / Edward Butscher.
Description: Lincoln: boxofchalk, 2017.
ISBN—13: 978-0999898208 (paperback).
BISAC: POETRY / American / General.

Local Lexicon

Edward Butscher

boxofchalk | LINCOLN/NOTTINGHAM/NEW YORK

for Paula and Amy forever

The poet is a god, or, the young poet is a god. The old poet is a tramp.
—*Wallace Stevens*

Contents

Acknowledgements

A number of the included poems appeared first in *Colere, The Coe Review, Confrontation, The East Hampton Star, Forge, The Georgia Review, Ginosko, The Ginosko Anthology 2, The Hat, House Organ, The Hiram Poetry Review, Home Planet News, Mobius: The Poetry Magazine, The Modern Review, Pacific Review,* and *Stray Dog.* The author extends his appreciation to the editors involved.

Abstract Expressionism

Beneath the head throb
a waterfall and nymphs
sing cream
fingers
at my chest, in my pants,
shafts of clotted ice
piercing heart
and penis.

This is delirium,
this vacancy,
a clawing at air,
life in abeyance,
head buried
in arms
that seem butter
from the lamp's atomic
glare, then sea foam,
as restless turnings
roll a bloated
carcass closer
to its brink.

I reside here, one
at a time, hanged
by sloth toes
till pain reams out
a taut stomach,
and I rise,
shuffling slippers

to the bathroom
where old piles ache
and bleed a garden,
a brilliant storm
of nothing but
Adam's first joy.

Objects, like remorse
for things unsaid,
people undone,
are defined
by their absence,

the stumble of loss
into explosive
color, green
and gold tiles
that slam my head
backward until I am
dizzy as a housefly.

A hole: a fire: a fetus
carved from loam,
African ebony
curved like a frog
nosing lily pads,
blooming mind
in holy water:

roses grown
around the steel
stem ideal of a rose,
thorny self-defense

2

from debris of other
poses, old enemies
who dip bandages
in tears, school
girls gutted
on creation.

Again, again,
(cannibal rite)
I suck in a tongue
then race to the throne
of vein-less butts far
from ordinary lives
beyond the opaque
window maze
where wives whistle
their lovers home,
and cats hump each
other hairless, a jungle
bled soft as clouds
before frozen
into art.

Animal Faith

In ancient Rome when
emperors aped Greek gods,
the infants of the poor
were flung on garbage heaps
as a necessary relief
from the circus of hunger.

Earlier still, by legend,
Spartan mothers left
their daughters and marred
sons to rot like sucked-dry
sunflower seeds
on salt-scummed rocks,
Nature's night soil
returned to the sea cave
where minotaurs first
bred a savior snake:

scripted beginning
of a grunting, greasy
olive-green machine
grinding down apple rinds
and graceless human waste
with steely ease.

Across the street from
St. Patrick's Cathedral,
a black fetus found rammed
down a trashcan mouth
like a scorched potato

remembers nothing
assumes everything.

I died twice before I died.
—Emily Dickenson

Artifice

Two weeks in a coma (so I learned)
after the second attack, there was
nothing but self, no world but mine,
before the hallucinations began
of a plan to persuade a German doctor
his mechanical device was deserved,
which would, at least, offer a motive
and narrative to sustain night turns.

I was alone, a bodiless eye pillowed
on icy white sheets and facing a huge
playing card, a jack of spades, if not
a king, glossy and obviously a work
of easel art, encased in clear plastic,
and I knew there was nothing else,
nowhere else, despair breathless
in the arctic air, now and forever.

Escape, breaking through, breaking
free, was all I could conceive, and
I bit down hard, savagely chewing
at the plastic sheath until parts of it
crumpled, cracked, collapsed into
the reality of a wallet's photo shield
that would not yield but held a hint
of surrender, emerging human faces.

I elided into a new place, a cement
basement storage area, confronted
by a familiar object, a rack of empty
metal shelves, painted garish green
and chipping, which I did not want
to touch or taste, though convinced
it had to be eaten, factory art at rest,
radiant under a fierce strobe light.

Nun-like priestess of the metaphor
Emerson had implanted at the storm
heart of atomic nature, Dickinson
was mistress to the dream that ensued
and endured as I plotted with hospital
cellmates to convey my worthiness
for a rebuilt engine, awakened daily
by a Nazi nurse's blackboard axioms.

I cannot remember when life dawned,
the pace-maker defibrillator installed
with methodical ease, surgeon voices
overheard reassuringly throughout,
until the cigarette-pack sized machine
hummed compact purpose, the art of it
restoring a heart's urge to devour light.

Astrology

It is an unversed universe I most fear
as it shrugs off unearthed trilobites
and a rust-scarred red wagon
with monstrous carelessness,
its small owner evanescing
in a mist off Flushing Bay.

Aubade

A distant ink dot of a spider
(what seems to be a spider)
suspended in neon-lit midair
by an invisible web and eye
above a white-tiled bathroom
corner like a dripped period

invites in all that is not there,
the ache and awe of galaxies
and their massively dawning
and dying planets and dwarf
stars below unslippered toes.

This is light's time and place
(elated at being here again)
to raise and praise the survival
of resurrected and regathered
selves, leaving behind night's
trite nightmares of old fears

and frayed lines of beloved faces
gone down forever under undone
expressions, reaching and holding
one another, another you, a boy
alone, daring a tree to drop him.

Bronx Zoo

They look. They look and laugh,
but her pitiless stare does not leap,

lacks the human weight of dancing
tiaras, an erne's pinpoint hunger
measuring an ocean's quick hares.

The ancient tortoise will not stir,
wills, instead, her pious watchers
to their scriptured dooms, a loss

of primal earth, whirlpool screams
unspooled from ritual rape scenes,
the mirror's covert silver deities

gurgled into unseen flames, curled
ghosts, billowy sheets of ash skin
flapping at her wire stalag, her air.

As if to speak, those sickle jaws
hinge wide, leak green phonemes,
howling without sound or pause.

They spin. They all spin inside
the diamond pivot of blind eyes.

Now, 'Which hand holds the brother?'
—*Simon Perchik*

Brothers

Near Troy, Catullus addressed
his brother's dumb remains
with a liar's lyric measures,
as if a poet's polished tears
could fertilize foreign soil
or spur a giant wooden horse
to again glisten and gallop
heaving flanks into a fall sun.

His ashes arrived in my absence
from California's Italian shore
(coffined in an urgent red, white,
and blue carton), now brooding
over a dust-sheeted TV altar,
far smaller than the boy I relive
with a ragged bundle of images
lashed together by the phone
lines of our last conversations
while he was sleeping in parks,
cardboard bonus-army shacks.

When Dali doubles our vision
with his crafty bifocal portrait
of a dead brother, construed
at a safe distance from dervish
shapes of a growing desert force,

beauty becomes entwined twin
strands braiding an eternity
that can never be combed free
of blood-bloated language lice.

He looked like neither of his
older brothers, nor anyone else
in the broken family rosary,
pious Aunt Mabel suspecting
an upside-down stomach clinic
doctors denied, his birth mark
(a dime of temple baldness)
echoing pursed lips as he sat
in the lap of Macy's Santa Claus
or posed, snowsuit squat, near
a candy-store rifled for friends.

Orphan of an insane mother
and a father's drunken dances,
he had a salesman's smiling guile,
baby-faced and babied by a senile
Nana, whose death completed him:

unspun helix of a human genome
that slithers through millenniums
of fires, storms, and retreating ice
with the caginess of a petted asp,
flying at a queen's naked throat
offered up as freely as two aunts'
refusals to press charges when he
emptied hearts and bank accounts.

At the end, after nursing two sisters
(tied into a single stick by reflex love
and eroded bodies), he headed west
to be shed of the avengers stalking
him in Flushing, a good boy at last.

I imagine heart beats of water beads
like stars in locket waves unleashed
by a beautiful young woman above
the clenched jaws of a marble mask,
who abandons me to heal her self
and avatars of the brother I house.

Laid side by side under concrete
slabs in the village near the Oise,
Theo and Vincent defy fiery wheat
fields of crows and cypress torches
as a melting gold watch palpitates
the midnight noon of my conceit
where I bid them all ave, ave, ave.

Caravaggio

Circling tourists, mainly American
and white-haired, are unable to dilute
its spotlight flood, the blood-letting
of a prone John the Baptist occupying
an entire wall in St. John's Cathedral,

his zealot's head bound for severing
to feed a reckless, feckless beauty—
or to float (strings invisible as shark
atoms) down to that sunless sea
of another poet's opium dream.

A docked white yacht bares masts
tall enough to recall the bristling
forest of Barbarosa's armadas
when Suleyman the Magnificent
twice gnashed his teeth against
Valletta's star-stoned bunkers,
awaits our return with champagne
cocktails and glazed tea cakes.

The caught faux knight fled Malta
to reclaim Rome's papal pardon
for his original crime, parading
rough trade across a Biblical stage,
painting the forbidden hidden light,
but he was wounded in the attempt,
fittingly dying of a fever at age 37.

Dance with me is the nightly request
as a school of mainly older bodies
surges around a rainbow-lit lounge,
childishly defying pain-jolted bones
and the fecal blackness smeared on
cabin portholes with a blind brush.

Chaos

I will it still in absentia
with the cowardice of a poet
caged by rag flesh and glass bone
when it scratches a frenzied alphabet
against the porch corner's cell walls:

the final quivers and glazed stare
of a feathered and beaked creature
dumped into this twilight life
from a teacup of darkness

only to be slashed back home
without ever growing large
enough to mother another

or streak through sun blasts
to snatch a briefer butterfly
from its immense mission.

Chinese Laundry

Pale tea-rose petals tremble a poem.

We dirty sheets
with our dreams'
torrid discharges
night after night.

For the terrorist
who smiles Irish lace
(fine lice-white lies),
a tumbling flake

has meaning,
bombs the eye,
shatters spectrums,
drilling obliquely
into crystal tears

and a river
that rushes away
from a woman's armless
teats and time stain.

A face collapses,
is swiftly folded
into a plaster flake,
a blade that dives,
divides stark facts.

I seam myself
in white fragments
on the wood floor,
fresh as starch trash.

After an apocalypse
of loveless armies
we dream at our throat,

the knife is a child's upraised hand.

Collateral Damage

The cloud engulfed a movie screen
in Main Street's grand RKO palace
like a "stupendous" erupting flower
after scenes of a howling bait dog
and classes of uniformed children
crouched under desks to save them
from a ferocious wind that tore
bodies out of skeletal homes,
x-rayed them naked of dreams.

Daily, we bear TV witness to ruins
in far cities difficult to pronounce
and piled corpses blown to tatters
by a teenager nursing a bomb at his
breast like a forbidden fox, or news
breaking out about schools ravaged
by lone gunmen intent upon fame,
laughing faces afloat in the crowd:
paper roses on a roadside cross.

A goose and the impressing brood
snaking so precisely behind her
across a dawn-hushed shore lane
almost elude the oceanic Lincoln,
but her last two goslings are struck
and ground into feathers as I curse
the pale aged driver in high quest
of bagels, who cannot feel the small
human carnage left in his wake.

Comedian

Dusk piles up luminous clouds
like rock-candy mountains
in the barroom mural
of a sentinel Indian
once adored:

our con artist
who jokes candy store
children into hunchbacks,
plugging peacock eyes against
stone mist, ripping atoms
from their sockets.

"It's raining birds, you turd,"
I warn him from above
the stage-high curb,
his body a flopped
domino kite,
paper pints
of California wine
broken in his cheeks,
dribbling baroque vines
across a half-gnawed chin
where foxes curl like snails.

He mumbles nothing but tar
babies, wordless as wire,
and I am glad to escape
his oily rainbow
disharmonies

20

as he waits
for winter
to bolt him fast
and paint the sentimental
strokes of a double-jointed
fall—where blundering
buffalo hordes left
only grins behind
white as spit.

Commercial Break

Wrapped in cellophane,
who can smell the inner
thighs that baked me pure
once upon a kneeling time?

The illusion is love,
a Wonder Bread truck
stalled at the curb.

Flames oven her nails,
my heart a sodden loaf
handled stale.

Too many girls but one,
the black-haired mute
who signed Italian
in crucified palms.

Making love,
breaking bread,
the driver has left for India.

There came unto me
that turned a tenderer voice for me.
—Thomas Hardy

Déjà Vu

Messages from the dead,
who clutter our closets
and sly bedroom corners
with whispers of dust,
are more cryptic than
the marble mausoleums
and plebian stone stiles
that mob Queens' green
hillsides like a grey army
of raised shields, besieging
Manhattan's bugle towers.

Or so I must believe,
their voices a chorus
around a moon-remote
woman when I lie down
for my afternoon nap
just before twilight wrings
me anxious, gelid Lucy
beneath me in her fluid
Hëloise guise, lips at work
on a pillow earlobe.

No wife calls from the grave
beyond the garden gate
nor boy (after escaping

mass) from a used-car lot's
unlocked Chrysler, where black
gospel songs rock its frame
to truant brothers' glee.
No baby sister sighs
over an unlived life, her
small blood sign scraped raw
by a languid ceiling fan.

Face down in defeat and
faux "noontide" desire,
I climax a stifled groan
that rumbles through an old
house to startle awake
a shelter kitten, she
alone sensing who walks
and is mourned here.

Dementia

Melodic are its three demonic syllables
pried from a deep Roman grave to root
in English hospitals and American labs
or dance like a pranked school skeleton,
serving as a noun escape, an anesthetic
for the last peeled-off sliver of self.

Crowned "Nana" by the family and tied
to a window chair by a foreign old age,
she cursed the grown daughters who
mothered her, changing her, feeding her
the Italian treats she loved to break down,
crumbling earth crusts into the silken oil
of remembered olive trees amid sliced
tongues of tomatoes and loud peppers.

"Aunt Ida" always, Edith winked coy smiles,
gave a girlish "yes" to whatever was asked,
efficient as ever only in the theatre of her
subway mind, where she wore a Red Cross
cape to tend the crowds of poor strangers,
crawling towards the infant she once was
without seeing the long distance behind.

A Polish Jew who fled as a boy to the wall
before settling in a New World and name,
"Yehuda Nir," swelled by a stuck ego's war
to save a self, he rose from a lost childhood
to heal fellow survivors, hating the tribe
that had hacked his father from his hand,
unable to forget or forgive or grow old.

Under eyelids blacker than any blackness
one can imagine or recall, it means raging
down the mind's spider-stitched staircase
to a cellar floor where pleasure was simple
as verse, now a night terror, like a Stoic's
scorned "death," that can't sleep or be.

Devotion

Blind son in her arms
(her bad medicine bag)
she leaped to the IRT tracks
landed between sizzling rails
as an express rocketed home,
floating, face-up, in a canal
where she had sunk before,
but surviving like a rat
whose barrel always breaks
under unexpected rains.

"Thank God, he's alive!"
the pasty Irish conductor
exhaled manure in her face,
potato-dense, ripened by faith,
tearing an aorta from her breast
with frantic canine hunger,
the son whose hat was lost
and whose wild eyes
would speak war.

Drone

Overheard in childhood's hiding place,
the voices of adults at a funeral feast
were indistinct from lack of Italian grace
after Nana and grandpa mumbled their last.

Hurled across intercontinental distances
by technicians unable to distinguish flesh
from the ice-sheen of machines or numbers,
the unheard drone splashes blood on steel,

smashes lumber spines, unlike the rockets
that screamed slamming into London homes
during the Blitz—blared over a parlor radio
as Nana hectored grandpa's clenched pipe.

Louder in echo ears when years descend,
they surgically prep us for silence's end.

Echoes

If an experiment can be repeated
it proves itself, as may a name sung
by steeple bells in a mind's Norway.

Language and consciousness echo
each another, a scholar reiterated.

I think I said I said I think I said I.

Edvard Munch's sequences of lovers
and screams and self-portraits (set
between a clock and Van Gogh's last

bed) retrace his global scream,
ringing out in cartoonish ripples

that ululate into a cosmic ocean.

Say it again, again and again, knees
exposed to rocks and shame in short
pants, finally shed for knickers, then

long pants, and a detached boyhood
of tulip trees and their visible roots

clawing at sky and armies of the dead.

Ordinary shapes paint in awareness,
walls, doors, women walking away
on high heels, repeatedly framed by

long slow days after broken nights
at the far end of an island and a life

that replicate what art once saved.

Electricity

I
Diagram real, its current exists only
when it powers machines, ceases
immediately upon being clicked
off, does not hemorrhage or scare
like lesions under healed skin.

Passion's literary and cinematic
symbol, it was used in *Frankenstein*:
a sensual nineteenth-century body
of felt knowledge, hoisted in a storm
to be raped by bolts of fractured life.

It invisibly cannons from nerve end
to nerve end in millions of tiny arcs
that synapse simpler memories,
reading the world that they project
in winding frames of perishable film.

II
Maker of static, I cross a thick
bedroom rug in the twilit glare
of finger flares that illuminate
an unmade and still empty bed
with scenes of childhood games.

Jagged as thrown mirror shards,
their incandescent fragments
pierce the solitude of an old age
that hoards the losses embraced
on artificial swan's down.

III
A sheeted woman's shapely form
descends through thunder shafts
of incendiary energy, discharged
for the sake of god-mad science
and art's Saturday holocausts.

Empedocles

The ocean heaves itself at a slack shore
it can never engulf.

Olympian peaks rip at pregnant clouds
like incisors of a galactic wolf.

The stars hammer an arrogant third eye
inside a narrow gash of turned earth.

But I alone impose human disorder
upon teeming subatomic mobs,

give voice to their vicious babble
with your whisper of desire,

teasing beauty out of night's marble womb
and into dawn's blood-engorged explosion.

Etymology

When a dreaming brain swells
there is nowhere for it to go,
its shield and eggshell art
against unnatural natural forces
door-less jail walls that squeeze
its prisoner into a fetal ball,
tormented awake and aware
by threats of a father's ax beak,
mothers devouring their young
to bury them womb safe

when lips first leaked *hell*.

Fallacy

The death of a child
(three or twenty-two)
by defect or overdose
stains backyard yew
trees spinach green
as they writhe
under the fists
of an August
downpour.

Foreign Affair

George Washington's ink-blot
profile remains
continental and unsolved

but as satisfying
as fresh white paste
freezing paper fast.

That summer
of our rendezvous

the Hungarian landlady
drowned below my sleep
in her own mud blubber

perhaps dreaming
of the flight from Hitler's
hurled black harpoon,

talons of starved oaks
scratching at
a drawn shade

all night long.

Hangover

Hunching through Main Street snow
and ice-honed winds near numb zero,
I laughed at the yellow taxi impaled
on the meridian's steel fence, not far
from a bulky woman taking photos
of her big Burberry-coated poodle.

My head a tethered balloon, eyelids
stabbed open by unseen icicles,
I wished I, too, were a teenager again,
striding inside seven-league boots
to shoulder cars free and shovel clear
the sidewalks of childless old couples.

Reading about Lorca the night before
(print too tiny and stomach tense as
a new basketball) after the phone
neglected to return a princess kiss
in the dark before dawn bleeds light,

I pictured a ditch beside any house
where all poets' bullet-seeded bodies
yearn to be thrown. As arrogant as
Dali was secretly shy, that laughing
deviant had spat his dreamt death
terror into the faces of the soldiers

who slaughtered for a pacifist Christ
frozen on his gold cross, convinced
they dare not kill and dump him
into a martyr's anonymous grave
where poppies and rebellions thrive.

I brutally stamp down infant hands
and stagger over monstrous breasts
(sour with unsuckled milk) to reclaim
a book-bricked studio that makes me
what I once was and will never be.

Heart

Nothing is an accident
in a poem or state of mind.
Nothing lacks design,
the craft of artisan hands.

This is the charm and chill
of a cosmos groaning on
an axis of stars without end.

After all, a sun's pulsating
chaos is not chaos at all
but the cauldron of a skull
dreaming astronomy.

An Aztec priest perched
on a leafless limb
like a sailor's parrot
and cawed what he never saw
about the human heart's
flight from itself:

the thunder of a hare
caught in dawn's gory jaws:

the first woman's sacred stillness
haloing a Catholic schoolyard
as it moved earth to erupt
with the drum rhythms
of an anchor love

when light angels appeared
to spear her tense thighs
into dancing tassels.

He was a liar then and now,
but his truth remains true

his phoenix wings
his golden bough
his burning bush

kindling pyre for the hearth
where we sacrifice the Other
for a taste of wrought beauty
that will outlive all appetites.

Heritage

We must let the imbecile live
if the daisy, caught in a sudden
frost, is to curtain the ocean's
horizon inside its saffron heart,

if that heart is to retain sidewise
mirrors in our single crystal eye
dauntless below a detonating sun.

Senseless impulses rooted in a white-
fenced garden amid jewel-case beetles
perfect minute sense (our senses in
things) and billow immense seraphim
wheeling mile upon mile of azure air.

Rocking on the porch of a tidy New
England house, the trim old lady—
however clenched or bitchy thin
beneath starched benevolent linens—
is the bearer of our traditions,
the brave tears she never sheds
fresh dew gilding flower hands.

And the exorbitant rates she charges
for her historic rooms and her new-
minted men are not too high a price
to pay for the wind that sighs out
of Plymouth Harbor like cow breath
to caress broken skyscraper faces.

History

Death erases all debts and duties,
even those due two spinster aunts
who rescued me from serial kills.
The heart-shaped CUTILLO stone
bears no word of their kind deeds.

This is my sour solace in the lit dark
when I lie alone, gagging on tongues.

From sleep to sleep, place to holy place,
I drive a boy's herd from East Hampton's
elm-harped aisles into the outlaw lair
of a Queens flat kept funeral-parlor neat
by adobe walls of ghosts and hymn racks
of rainbow books that can muscle aloft
a concrete vault equal to any sky-gutting
cathedral spire or tower's babbling thrust.

Knowledge is agony refluxed when I
learn from a porter's overheard chatter
that Flushing's giant weeping beech
(opposite John Bowne's beached house)
had been butchered behind my back,

plowed into Earth's pyramiding mounds
of skulls and jig-sawed spines as easily
as glossy photos of People are flipped
in a doctor's waiting room—or a moth
slammed between pages of a St. Mary's
textbook to beard a stone president.

Aping Hamlet's exhilaratingly savage stab,
I embrace what is more than I to slam me
against heaven's sun and iron gate, kissing
your elegant hands free of my guilt stains.

This must underlie our love, my love:
the mole mouth of a ferocious hunger
burrowing down denim-tensed thighs
in quest of a fur pocket below thought
before sensually slim limbs shiver shut
in a spasm recall of earlier incursions

and the rowdy, restless root fingers
slithering inside an unloosened bra
to paw minutely mute nipples taut
as prayer-shellacked worry beads
or lips of an embalmed boy king.

These feral legions are not, I argue
(with a playfully inchoate croon for
atonement over a bare belly altar),
poised, host-thick, on Mongol steppes
to ravage your lushly cultured fields
even while wetting you in tribal cries
that stiffen between us as they dry,
erased before knowing is known.

Death smashes autumn air into spikes
of asbestos or malicious anthrax spores,
fired from a male forge I do not need
to ignite and mount the avalanche threat
of ash extinction that throttles each throb
of light after you leave me for tomorrow.

Irony

The morning struggle to focus
a brain's transparent eyeball
after escaping (yet again)
the death one can never imagine
when alive is the crutch distance
that compensates us with art
enough to span dark matter.

Jewish builder of a Christian
universe, born blind in Gaza's
unchained eternity, Einstein
was forced by vulture-hearted
Nazis to flee Viennese circles
for suburb-square New Jersey,
there to see his fierce desert god
collapse into quantum laughter.

Kindergarten

When a goldfish floats
the country wings home
on a windshield's moth debris.

Cows and crab-apple trees
and fences of green alfalfa
fall flat as a linoleum floor

without scent or sense.

Rows of corncob canoes
dangle, naked, from gobs
of school paste and paint

without taste or taste

rag parents fluttering
furtively away as a child
circles a mulberry bush

without kiss or ken.

La Petite Morte

Green vase on a white doily
squeezes window light
into lime juice

blood of a dinosaur, desert
cheeks like a caked
sea floor, cheese
smiles.

An infant's skull, even if unreal,
can be x-rayed by laser eyes
to unlace a Mississippi's
imploring
eels.

Danger lurks here like a locked
mind in a room that reeks
of empty wine bottles,
lipstick wounds,
perfumed
books.

I father an unbearable lightness.

Mathematics

Poets, of course, should be unlimited,
more divine than any computer
in their profane arrogance,
ruthless but playful
as a mousing cat.

This was an interior calculation,
the calculus under my shout.

And yet, there is talk of numbers
that are not real, which I
cannot assimilate,
refuse to imagine
believing numbers are always real
as oranges, trains, Calder mobiles,
that being real is what makes
them numbers.

Unreal numbers dare not exist, unlike
Blake's tiger, which continues
to believe in itself, grinning
(oak-wise) at the crime
of dark energy.

If unreal numbers do exist, and the best
authorities, the incomprehensible
ones, insist they do, plentiful
as slum rats, then I am
afraid for the first
time, wondering
where it will
all begin.

Only one thing in art is valid,
that which cannot be explained.
—Georges Braque

Muse

The screaming old lady razored in the park:
streets soften, hold me fast as a smashed
beetle to her tar-smooth breasts:

she loomed lily smoke,
a dwarf friend,
opening in rings of faked pleasure
to lasso blunt swords
back into stone:

swollen like legend
my voracious briar.

I know you now,
the wilds you wire
the felines you devour
the bud of paradise petrified
in the past's space-warped cave.

What remains? Bones? Wisps of hair?

Words are tiny markers on a mirror
page, curdling machine-gun germs,
as the corpses collapse
into cigar ashes
stains of salt.

I once believed in small cartons of milk
that chuckled as I arched them empty.

New Age

A vole's plush cream breast
stained by a red dirt smile
held in a quivering hand
gives Death a bad name.

Nursing Home

Another hanging connection,
another gutteral whisper
near the lip of hysteria
above the tidal suction
of her unsure being

as I wake, again drenched,
from adolescence's dream
of the island girl in jeans
a paradox of lean and lush
like that Ukrainian skater

simulating foreplay's coy
pouts and poses and painted
fingers and mouths, licking
hair from cheeks and chest
swallowing strawberries
in a single giggling gulp.

"My apartment! My apartment!"

A naked radiator whistled
in the Smart Street apartment
where a mother's waxing breast
launched another's moon ride.

I see myself in the sly fright
of paranoid eyes so wide
they multiply childhood's
appetite for immortality.

"They're stealing our home!"

She laps at me like a cat
atop an unexpected fetus,
tonguing broken leg veins

to the scar near my heart
where three roads converge
when a ribcage collapses
into thrown pick-up sticks

the throat of silence loud
as a hidden universe's
wheezing black holes.

Original Sin

To mistake a plump breast for eternity.

A brother's head is fantasized smashed
against a boulder or the carton of his
ashes stomped into real Hampton dirt
not far from cherished feline remains.

To snake free of a soused father's
swamp embrace, willing him dead.

A neighborhood girl was deflowered
by teenage animals, my "I" immune
to her sullen proffer of torn petals
and wounded, wet-dream roots.

To rifle a maiden aunt's secrets
in a shameful underwear drawer.

At the last, arbitrary as the poetics
of this, punishment and penance
compass an enormous separation

curling, fetal-taut, against a bedroom
wall, cradled in the voluptuous arms
of a mother tongue, laboring to calm
this old man's death-rattled heart.

Overture

Just outside my radar-large tin ears
jazz played against the rock and roll
thumpings of a teen from the fifties
obsessively chasing his jalopy girls.

Louis Armstrong occupied Corona,
and Lionel Hampton was in Flushing
then, his xylophone yard backing on
the park where stickballs cannoned,

his sexy wife returning our Spaldeens
with an indulgent smile and hip hint
of middle-class romance in the curves
drawn to a wall's chalked black box.

One hand on the wheel, he replayed
black and white bodies back into clay.

Paranoia

It is a quiet, noisy, injured thing
chained inside a forehead's theatre,
streaming star performances of people
who can never be touched or trusted.

It is murder by degree and decree,
a Dutch or Russian uncle, predator wise,
Stalin's problem-solving gulag slaughters,
as if death alone could annihilate death.

It is a furtive, infantile rage clenched
in a father's quick fist like graveyard dirt
or hidden roll of coins, his wife listening
to a cold radio for plots against their son

Philosophy

Like people and other animals,
galaxies tend to cluster in herds,
their enormous secret mass the weight
of human terror that a black hole
will suck in brain and heart
without idea or love.

I feel the iceberg gravitas of death
press me down upon the cream waves
of you with a panic as old as a boulder
forever shouldered up a hill—until

we break apart and bend together
again in an orbit of fever words,
clutching opposing positions.

Pigeons

A dark, lean, hard man who spoke little,
forever hatted like a taxicab driver, his
childish smile rare as a peacock unfolding
below the flock of pigeons that exploded
from upturned palms like electrified stones,
his form distinct above us on a tenement roof:
a foreign saint set against rabid clouds.

He was our uncle, we were informed, but
he never looked at us, shy as a Dutch tulip,
and my father said in secret (man to man)
that he was a cousin from the family's wild
branch where blood seethed with syphilis
bugs and was thin enough to candle eggs—
his wife a balloon shape sloped over a kitchen
window chair who could not bear children.

It was on the Lower East Side, just after the war,
when we first glimpsed him and his pigeon host
and I guessed from the way my father gauged
his rooster frame that he was unique, a specimen
divine in the madness propelling him into the sky
each morning, a laugh like startled mallards as he
unlatched the wire door and slowly pivoted on tar
in tune, in time, to circling shafts of darkness.

Near the end of their lives, my father and he sat
side by side in a urine-stained couch to monitor TV
soap operas. Teeth gone, nearly deaf, he did not stop
clucking as they sipped headless beers, reciting

newspaper horror tales by rote—fried infants, raped
nuns, tortured cats—asking if I had ever tasted
"a coon hair pie" or rode in a rumble seat.

At my father's wake, he slumped alone in the back
and played with himself, cave grin bearing witness
to the betrayal of our shared laughter, and soon he
was also dead, his wife dancing in a nightgown
on the griddle of a snow-ribbed street as black
attendants handled him gently into an ambulance,
dawn horizon bleak as a tossed purse, pigeons
ascending like tattered angels from my awe.

Practice

I
To make a poem when old enough
to simulate the corpse you will make
demands daily muscular practice,
molding mirror shapes dense enough
to resist increasing acid erasures.
Metaphors trip a child's vest bomb
or etch a black cat dropping mouse
organs like stained pearls on a rug.

II
Mrs. Palmer's rows of echoing zeroes
were penned with fourth-grade zeal
to flood black marbled notebooks
with waves of beauty and control.
Similes now flower from roots deep
in an aging brain, snowy with plaque,
where a yard horse walks into a wall
like a sad-eyed mother gone mad.

III
Three tight stanzas, satisfying
as Hegel's Greek-slick dialectic,
must hoist an enormous universe
terrifying as a foreseen darkness,
but space debris cannot contrive art
without a dead brother's small smile
or the stained robes of polar bears
haunting broken glacial altars.

Proteus

After another pensioned day, the dream
rips at my chest like a clutched wolverine,
slashing me into a field of pine skeletons
battle-decapitated near a sludge current
tumbling too swiftly to float survivors.

I flounder in mud without legs and arms,
terrified by a helplessness acres below
metaphor, childhood's cinema horror:

a black circus freak with an infant body
wrapped in burlap like a peanut grub
writhing toward tented light and grave.

I wrench myself awake with sweaty will
pinned under a sun's tons of gorgeous swill.

Punctuation

When computers democratized
capitals and i-pods abridged words
themselves, deathless prose died
a billion deaths, tiny as pricks
in a condom—and no less perilous

Doomed to knowledge of erasure
at an early age by sudden shifts
of scenery and regal personae
(mother, father, nurturing aunts),
which meant predicating subjects
into objects at some felt remove
(brutal as brackets) from a child's
steeple-high Emersonian eye,

the boy platformed castles at his
two Catholic elementary schools
from the sentences diagrammed
with an obsessive cardinal joy,
raising praised context and conduct
ramps under the weight of Latin's
imported stage directions.

After college degrees and teaching
confirmed its value, a semi-colon's
dragnet sweep had the raft appeal
of rescuing second and third ideas
from history's enormous annals,
of elaborating revisions and subtle
eddies into carpets of The Master
and transfigured dream lovers.

Simon the Poet harpoons his colons
at the other side of the great divide
between conscious and unconscious
space, releasing fresh oxygen back
into the vacuum separating equals,
a mind expanding in a fecund, if
uneasy, way, unearthing old levels
of lore below remorseless stones.

But periods remain the most satisfying
to execute, reaffirming a sentence's
existence at the acme of completeness
even as it concludes, like a Hemingway
story, on death's implacable sword,
and it is difficult not to love them, no
matter what is obliterated, a sequence
of cats and dogs, whom I would have
saved if I could, like a jaded Casanova,
or the boyhood friends who never
said goodbye in words or a lost shout.

The end, in the end, is all there is.

Reflux

In the latest bedroom scenario
from an aged poet wrapped in
his wet winding sheets, the limp
end of all lyric utterance dangles
from a slack-jawed bedroom door
like a blood-flowered tuxedo shirt
(black satin tie puddled below)
after a shellac-filmed family brawl
as impossible to ingest as infinity
or my own sourly rehearsed death.

Rehabilitation

Wonder if you recognized me waving
at you atop our high German wheels
as Sunday morning swells of shore light
again swept Stevens from his dump site.

Two aging lady artists hiking by the sea
above naked dunes and sordid grassy
clumps, evoking, via a bicycle construct,
the tall, elegant girl in the gym, strutting

her ballerina form and beauty, lofty breasts
and thighs muscling up self-consciousness
as if performing solely for the voyeur eyes
of an old poet sprawled across his ashy sky.

Hospital dreams compel dusk redactions
in cold pursuit of a bleeding abstraction.

River Styx

Teeming schooling multitudes
of our species have evaporated
since we first lumbered ashore
to surge in herds down history.

An ark artistry is water as womb
and womanhood as amniotic sea

tasted in childhood after lessons
on Christ and unjust original sin,
sheets sweated sour in the night,
soaked in images of deathless
death, unreeling serial absences,

gas chambers everywhere, sewers
enough to suck down human waste,

a once-mad mother, tamed fuzzy,
falling in a joyous rose bathroom
after decades away from home
to swirl down a shower drain,

a father behind a curtain mask
slitting the throat of a prisoner
in a 3rd Avenue barroom screen,
the black blood of it drunk white.

Charon is shaded mist, a mournful
shadow, steering nothing into myth
to shield us from the nothing ahead.

Ruins

Piranhas are near mythical fish,
their smallness of teeth and size
intrinsic to the terror they inflict,
their swarming ferocity evident
in their victims' quicksand fate:

a human carcass stripped down
to a skull tabernacle in a ribcage
temple, spinal stairway spiraling
inside an alabaster palace before
swallowed by a seething Amazon.

It was at Ephesus where we moved
slowly down dirt streets amid fields
of milky ruins behind a corpulent
English couple, sweaty but cheerful
as they labored to keep up with our
pretty Turkish guide, whose rainbow
umbrella and girlish chatter herded
us through gardens of spilled marble,
most impressed by two theatres and
the Library of Celsus's intact façade.

Aristotle, tutor for Alexander, who
conquered Ephesus, taught the value
of collecting specimens to assemble
the skeleton science must flesh whole.

The only ghosts were absent scrolls
and sunken traces of younger selves.

Salvage

How deep is the dive into a crumpled
sea, retrieving wreckage of voyages
lost to weather and human ambush?

Between bathroom and vestibule
tokens everywhere, hoarded and spilt
over a sleek surface indifferent to them
(globe, Italian coins, a charm bracelet)
cluttering a bureau saved from a wife's
first marriage, florescent color photos
of unmet nephews and nieces (now
grown), a dead uncle young in teacher
shirt and tie, immigrant parents nearby
in their grimly formal 1950s dotage,
my own face a stranger's public smile
scissored from a school's tailored year.

If synaptic connections are thickened
or unlearned by experience, how firm is
the web binding axons to their ghosts?
Rescuing the personal past, what I loved
and was, seems anxiously frail in light
of a slashing, mote-clouded shaft of sun—
unsteady hands dusting off a glassed
picture of a grinning boy in a marine's
dress uniform (prematurely discharged)
or bleached spines of books stacked
in a hall closet of memorabilia, as if
they could jetty tame a torrent of voices
and overheard hospital consultations.

Across the front page of a tall morning
newspaper, a line of redbush saplings
encircle a New Mexican square in honor
of recent Spartans: bagged, tagged, and
flown home from a moon of mangled
bodies—to be reassembled in a desert
garden's unseasonably eternal paradise.

Seasonal

In the green egg
of a nursing oak
I sense the sinew urge
of a resurgent spring,
fingering its lizard skull
like a miniature mine
left behind
by the war

while remembering
that morning journey
into her wrecked mind
where demons wore white—
weaned from her bed
by love and a need
to be relieved
of her needs.

In the mouths of blossoms
I smell urine-bleached
petticoats, her flaccid
loins rain-plumped
worms underfoot.

Past silent houses
and green carpets
of this Flushing town
she never understood,
I plowed her
feather weight

wishing bell peppers
and tomato tongues
could sound our breaths.

Older than she,
a porch-proud friend
sat smug above
our slow passage,

defending her soil
with rag-flagged sticks
waving goodbye
waving goodbye
like whips of gull wings
lacerating sun-lit air.

In restless fragments
of the sky's broken

shell, in clumsy wing heaps
hacking at heaven's bodice,
(I hear her climb)
grandmother vine.
"Mama mia!"
she sang aloud
like a lost child

or was it "Eddie"
she accused
as the axis of her wheelchair
groaned from the earth,
turning on hollow
catacomb bones?

The ghost of a barber
husband was a calla lily
haloing her maize-fine hair
when the glasshouse winked,
smiled, swallowed her whole.

We left her there
I leave her there
one maple-tense day
each returning spring
without even a donkey
to bray her home

or root up the stranger
who plants her there to die.

Senescence

Read in Latin class with a witty,
polio-lamed professor, Cicero's
essay on old age from his final
year is retrieved to anatomize
the unhappiness he phrased as
retirement, as enfeebled body,
lost physical pleasures, and ken
of these as the last step to death.

Memories are precise (real or
not) in their details, precious
in the blood-intensity of their
scenes: an enclosed sun porch
of a large Dutch-colonial house

where it is now possible to will
(no longer a shy, chubby child)
myself inside a gaunt grandfather
in stiff white shirt and black tie,
reaming a crusted pipe before
shakily tamping Prince Albert
ashes as a senile wife in a floral
housecoat curses him for her
crumbling body and brain.

When Antony's soldiers caught
up with Cicero as he fled in a
litter (frail beyond his 63 years),
he silently thrust out his head
for their swords to strike off.

Skeleton Key

I
"Like madness, paradoxes
fascinate the sanest of mortals."

A mortarless Daedelus rendered blind
under winding sheets of belief, uniform
truth, until exiled, interred, still raving
over the chaos of tower ruins.

II
Shorn of limbs, worm breath, feather
enigmas rise, bone by cat-gnawed bone.

Turning in the rusted heart of a robin,
the key cannot revive him,
halt their ascensions,
hush their singing.

III
Is there a break, a crack of sense,
in the iron logic of its great chain,
some maw or star to pry open or shut?

IV
Weakened by seasonal phlebotomies,
the weight is always from jailor keys,
hunching shoulders, slackening jaws,
the sullen law of human centuries
locked in de Sade's slimed cells.

V
Turning, turning, with a febrile hand,
are these, too, lost classroom refrains?

Trope

The phenomenal raven perched on Poe's bust.
The voyeur raven caged inside Kafka's name.
The rain-enameled crow refusing to be scared
off a severed cat carcass that asbestos dawn
I drove back into Queens for another funeral.

United States

When the mother was swept
from the overwhelmed suv,
her two babies (strapped in
the back seat for safety's sake)
swallowed the entire river,
gallant strangers on its bank
running and leaping for
hanged bundles of sky.

Wonderland

The old golf course was deserted
and had been since the 'thirties,
weeds surging across its flanks
like preambles of a broken dam,
splintered flag rafts of brambles
clogging its hidden veins.

He led her by the hand
to the cave of earth he had dug
and covered with Autumn leaves
when still a Green Mountain Man
before they sat and pretended
to sip their pretend tea.

Alice poured and chided him
for forgetting how to hold a cup,
but he could not stop shaking
and caused the sullen clouds
to blunder into a storm.

"We'll be drenched!" she squealed
in panic, laughing all the while,
as they hugged one another
like an old family pair.

He pulled down her panties
and kissed the nest place
where it hurt so she could not
fly or fall in again.

The blood of it was not profound,
this laying on of childish hands,
but healing came, scab-hard,
to scar all our blonde days.

Zeno

Before the clock-radio intones
its redundant, abundant
catastrophes,
I rise,
I think,
and shuffle carefully
through the shrouded house,
shaking off sticky threads
of hushed people and rooms.

I Braille-read hallway walls
and rely upon a kitchen's
radiant calculating eyes
to feed resurgent cats

before defecating
in comic relief.

Zero

Moses' eyes concave
into zealot blindness
that makes stone burn,
cold flesh grow green.

Serpent as a piece
of red bakery string
dropped on a bed,

blinking unblinking
at the sepia smiles
of alien relatives,

the old woman's
cancer-sour tongue
paints her bedroom
the color of corn.

This is my crime.
Survival is hers.

A robin's blank eye
mimics a sun nugget
set so still amid vague
fluff carnage of its
wingless remains:

the beauty of a thing
that once had breath,
being and beauty

fused into a tear
for cupped hands
to catch intact

buffed perfect
between artful lids.

www.ingramcontent.com/pod-product-compliance
Lightning Source LLC
LaVergne TN
LVHW011410080426
835511LV00005B/468